Thin Places

Thin Places

JOHN CROSSLEY MORGAN

RESOURCE *Publications* · Eugene, Oregon

THIN PLACES

Resource Publications
A Division of Wipf and Stock Publishers
199 W. 8th Ave., Suite 3
Eugene, OR 97401

www.wipfandstock.com

ISBN 13: 978-1-60608-186-0

Manufactured in the U.S.A.

For Cynthia, with love and gratitude

Contents

Part II: On Life and Living

PREFACE

IT WAS DURING A TRIP to England and Wales with my two brothers that I learned what the Welsh mean by the words "thin place." I had been taking a morning walk down a path outside the Tintern Abbey in Wales when I discovered a rather small but sprawling tree, its branches creating what seemed to be a safe place under which travelers might rest. I crawled under the branches and sat quietly to watch the morning sun break across the ancient abbey sky. It did feel safe and even sacred, a place to go to rest and reflect upon the mystery of life. Sitting there, I felt the presence of others who had rested there before, and who knows, perhaps the same Spirit which the poet Wordsworth felt when he took walks with his sister above the path winding above the same abbey.

Later, over lunch, I spoke with a local resident and told him my story about sitting under that old tree. He looked at me and said quietly: "It's called a thin place." I had never heard the words before, so he patiently explained that a thin place is very special where you felt a presence so deep and mysterious that you needed to stretch language to describe it. He explained that a thin place could be a location in nature or in the presence of others, and it could be either awe inspiring or terrifying. "That sounds like a description of poetry," I laughed. "Maybe that's why the Welsh are such good poets," he said with a twinkle in his eye, later confiding that he wrote poetry himself.

In the months ahead I became more aware of "thin places" in my life, whether in my backyard garden or by a river or in the presence of another person and even sometimes in moments when I felt awe or fear during a thunderstorm. And I came to understand that once you feel the power of thin places you tend to see them under many circumstances (with people or in places you might have missed). And more surprisingly, I learned that when you carry a thin place in your mind and heart, you can go there whenever you feel the need, as Wordsworth did in London when he recalled daffodils growing elsewhere. I even practiced conjuring up a thin place before I was wheeled into surgery--the scenes from a Welsh countryside in front of me rather than the white gowns of nurses and doctors. It brought me strength to face whatever might come.

Who knows, perhaps a thin place might also be those dimensions which separate the living from the departed, which some report as "near death experiences," where the veil between dimensions is lifted if only briefly? I have learned that a thin place is the soil out of which poetry grows.

The poems collected in this little book are about such places and people and times in my journey through life where the veil separating the reality in front of me is temporarily lifted to catch a fleeting glimpse of what is just over the horizon.

John Crossley Morgan

Part I

On death and dying

SLIPPING

The world is slipping. So am I, back to my roots
where the double-fisted circuit rider drank and prayed
for his listeners to stay out of hell.
My grandfather spoke of sin until it crawled
down your pants and flopped exhausted on the floor.
Those were the days, he says, when sweet Jesus would arrive
to seize you by the throat and shake you dry.
My aunt said he fled to Iowa to preach salvation
to crusty farmers and northern rejects, then died
and was buried on some lonely hill.
My other grandfather, more refined, sipped tea flavored
with whiskey, and with his golden tongue
later unlocked the doors to the kingdom.
My world is slipping away, too. I wonder who will
save me from a hell no one believes in anymore?

FOR GRANDFATHER

Time is short.
Eternity is long.
Sail on, sail on.
The sea is vast,
the crossing short.
Sail on, sail on.
The ocean wide,
the storm is brief.
Sail on, sail on.
Home, home at last,
the journey's done.
Sail on, sail on.

TO MY FATHER

The pulpit seems bare now, the sanctuary deserted.
There is no need for further exposition.
Above Broad Street the grey steeple
Stretches, crying to the sky.
This day you are no longer here
And I, without a text, must mourn.
And we are children, living within time.
And we are children, looking for a sign.
But what sign would you give to us?
A measured voice, your English lyric?
A father's hand, our essential delight?
I think perhaps the laughing eyes
That saw the joy of every moment.
Now you, who ministered to others,
Must pray for us,
Who suffer such a loss.
Somewhere, deep among familiar stars,
I know you hear.
Your gifts of words, and of The Word,
You gave them freely,
And lost them in the heat of life.
And we live to speak them, hear them,
Write them, have them, be them.
No living word ever dies
But is transported back to life.

Dear Father, here thy servant keep,
As shepherds gather in their sheep;
Home, home at last, his days are done
And now the final victory won.

TO MY MOTHER

Mother, if I had known how you wept
in closets, I would have come;
but you wept quietly for forty years
and died, hardly remembering your name.
We die the death we deserve, some say;
but you never deserved this shaking death.
Mother, I will remember for you now:
the long train rides to Denver where you amused
the crowd with stories of the bald headed man
or life in sin-free Indiana,
or the long nights you sat by my bed
wondering if I would survive the summer.
You may rest at last.
My poetry is yours, really; my gentleness, too;
my loyalty, your legacy; my sadness, too.
Women: Listen to this one man-child:
 Do not forget your names.
 Do not always live for others.
 Live for yourself while you can
 and we will call you blessed.

FOR MY SISTER

The seagull sits and stares.
I don't know what she sees
as she sits perched upon a post
above the rushing sea.
The seagull barely moves,
her wings I cannot see.
But if I wait and watch
her eyes are watching me.
Does she spot the ashes left
to drift upon the sea,
the only part remaining
of my sister, dear to me?
Or is she heaven bound
out through the open door,
to rest at last relieved
upon some distant shore?
O God, who keeps the tides
and makes the water toss,
wait patiently for her and us
who suffer such a loss.

LINES NEAR TINTERN ABBEY, WALES

Two years have past since you departed, and I set sail
to the harbor of our ancestral faith, not sure
where I am heading or if anyone would be there.
It hardly seems possible you are gone and I am left
to wait the morning break alone.
Here by some ancient wall of a ruined faith
I see the dew melt as sun bursts. The mists
dissolve to golden glow as day ends.
Before me the abbey is still, the monks gone.
Time serves its need of turning everything to dust.
The light falls to earth, while white birds soar,
as if angels announcing the empty tomb.
By the River Wye I have felt a Spirit deeper still
that winds through our lives, unheralded journeys
above the blue heavens, white clouds, green
loveliness where death has fled.

FOR JIM REEB*

Count the carnations on my table corner,
white as the snow outside,
light as their pedals falling to the ground.
Count them, one by one, they fall away
as did you, one cool March day,
but not so gently and not without a cry.
Some say it takes a martyr
to make a movement.
But, O Lord, why so many gentle people
gone to graves?
And still we kill.

*Rev. James Reeb was a pastor who was brutally killed in Selma, Alabama, March 1965, after a civil rights march.

A PSALM FOR MARGARET

O God, I have cried unto you.
My whole being has sought you out.
O God, I have wrestled with you;
In my pain I cry to you for help.
In my weakness I seek your strength.
If I cry out, will you hear me?
If I weep, will you dry my tears?
Be like a mother to me, gather me in your arms.
Be like a father to me, protect me from evil.
Our days, they seem as deepening shadows
Casting darkness in the land;
Our moments, like grass, wither in the sun.
Send light, O God, and let us live.
Send light, O God, and let us live.
No creatures lives but that she dies;
No flower blooms, nor tree, nor plant.
O God, we do not ask for more than these:
The strength to bear the pain.
Your presence in the evening star,
And glad praise when day is done.
Praise life that in us grows,
For time and toil and love,
For every moment of our days
For what we are is yours.

CRUCIFIXION

They hung a shark upon a stake,
drove two nails through the hard skin,
pointed the fins upward,
as if a prayer for mercy.
They claim fish feel nothing,
but who took pleasure
in this naked agony?
The Massachusetts Bay is calm;
the yachting club full of gin
and summer sailors.
From a window, across the beach,
the outline of a cross is covered soon
by crowds of seagulls,
wings beating madly,
rejoicing in his death.

AT EASTER TIME

At Easter time you feel it most,
the loss of someone gone before,
as if you could rejoice at all—
though everyone else thinks otherwise.
You only know the emptiness
of hollow hymns and rituals
and sermons full of platitudes.
Every closet tells a tale,
every item brings to mind
the memory of a loss so deep
that all you want to do is sleep
away the waking hours
and dull the dread you feel inside.
The prayer is simple, said anew:
Let me make it through the day.

IN THE PASTOR'S STUDY

In the pastor's study the books on mercy and grief
Line the walls.
But he is cold.
Turn your deaf ear on me, cleric.
Practice the learned smile, the nodding head
Which you've trained so well.
Turn your cold heart my way and listen.
I am dying.
The sentence was dying. There's no question about that.
The sentence was crying. There's no question about that.
The sentence was trying to live again.
There's no question about that.
Then why do you sit so rehearsed?

A BLOCK AWAY

A block away is another world
with new ways to measure time.
There is no noise in the morning.
Nights are dark and cold.
Being alone without clocks
opens up the vastness of space.

FEAR AND TREMBLING

You stand alone in Wannamaker's store,
lost for a moment from your mother.
The bronze eagle stares down at you, waiting.
You hope he has eaten.
At least then you knew the contours of fear
and stopped trembling when you heard
the soft voice of your mother calling your name.
These days such moments last longer,
stopping you dead in your daily tracks.
Nameless vapors crowd within.
Reason isolates itself and works on you,
shaping life into ghostly, gray forms.
Some adults, we who seek the eternal mother,
only to release more anxiety into the world.
The universe is devoured by our fears and we
call it religion.

NO-MAN

Particles of water on the rock's edge
poised to drop. They just hang there, waiting
for who knows what.
I am no-man, nowhere left to go,
unattached, in mid air, waiting to fall
into another space.

NEXT TIME

Next time he will be mad; I know it.
For the message the first time
came without his being violent.
It was more of an announcement:
The time is now to choose,
You cannot serve two masters.
You must love until your arms ache
and your heart breaks
and then love more.
No more the streams, the sky, the sea.
No more the brothers, the sisters.
The cosmos will shrink
to fit on a pinhead.
And only the spirit will be left
to brood upon nothing in particular.

WHEN IT COMES TIME TO DIE

This morning I fed the sparrows gifts of seed
recalling one man who said God cared for them.
I'm not so sure. I've found too many
frozen creatures lifeless on the barren ground.
But I'll be generous and cast seeds anyway
just like the power my father said ruled heaven.
As still as the fallen snow I sneak outside
and hide behind an evergreen.
A minute passes. Then one by apprehensive one
like supplicants before an altar, these sparrows land—
and skip across the silver walk to feed.
I watch in wonder how their little choir
swings and sways in boisterous, playful song.
Such Pentecostal joy they have that I cover my ears
as my feet start moving and my hearts resounds.
If I acted like this in church they'd have the ushers
lead me out.
They'd be hushing and slithering all the way
down their tasteful aisles.

My neighbor has been watching me.
She says she knows more loss than gain,
and wants to know why I bother.
Who am I to argue? She speaks from eighty years
of losing everyone she loved.
She speaks with authority. I have only hints

and guesses about everything.

I know I cannot save all these tiny birds.

But I can scatter seeds in hope one or two survive.

And if I make light the burdens of their beating hearts,

in heaven's eye that may be enough.

Perhaps one day He will offer me a few remaining seeds,

so that I , too, may soar on wintry winds

when it comes time to die.

Part II

On life and living

BORA DA*

Bring on the spring, I cannot wait much longer
for the bursting of the flowers or the swaying of the stream.
Sun bright and moon beam, daylight and evening teem
with such life and childish shouts that my heart outlasts
this cold and blighted winter gray.
Bring on the spring. I've had enough of ice and snow.
Bring on the spring. I've had enough of death
and dying and all things that seem to me
lost and buried under vault and key.
Let there be sprouts of green and budding plant
and all that makes my soul to sing.
My Celtic spirit, trapped in time, awakes again
to sing an ancient rhyme: "Bora da! Bora da!"
Bring on the spring. I'm ready to be reborn.
Bring on the spring. I'm ready to play.
This game of life is deep in me,
Deeper than the sea is wide and sky is blue,
and closer still to God than my own breath
which sounds in me each time I wake:
Bora da! Bora da"!
Bring on the spring. It's time has come.

*From the Welsh, meaning "good morning."

LOVE

Only old people with wrinkles and arthritis
know about love.
It's all worth saving
when everything else is gone.
Grown taunt by disappointments
the body awaits the end
and can no longer melt under lover's heat.
Only dying persons find each day
a lifetime,
for that is all that's worth finding.
Facing death makes love everything.

CHURCH TIME

The hour is near. I need to rush to
church and worship whatever God shows up.
But daffodils shoot yellow flares
above the barren ground,
and call to me a different tune:
Come out and play, come out and play
and bow before the morning sun
to hear the songs of doves above
and smell the morning breaking new.
The hour's close, I need to rush.
But now I rise from bended knee
from marveling at the buds and grass
like saviors sprouting from the dead.
They call to me a different verse—
Sing praises for another day.
The hour's now gone. I still am here.
This golden god of morning blends
into the springing day.
What pagan soul within me lurks to
take delight in ancient oaks and mist
upon the earth?

Ah, thanks be to whatever gods there are,
in this green grove, under this small tree,
that I can feel so alive.
This is about as close to heaven
as any Welshman ever gets.

TRINITY

I think that I shall never see
An end to fights over trinity.
Is one in three or three in one?
One God, with spirit and with son?
My simple mind cannot debate
These attributes of heaven's fate,
Nor can from these a meaning weave
Consistent with the Nicene creed.
Too many gods, too much to view
From this, my simple wooden pew.
If three is one, and one is three,
Then where is God and which is me?

ANDOVER NEWTON

They give us bad press here,
for we are the sons and daughters of Jebediah Morse
who condemned us to hell.
They think us stuck above our necks
With smirks upon our lips
and witty sayings to share.
But one day the inward law will rule
and there will be no need for learned doctors.
On that day creeds collapse and we shall sit
together for that holy communion
around whose table everyone is welcome.

A PRAYER

Lord, continue to keep yourself
from those who take lightly your name:
The hustlers of cathedrals and endowments,
rich, young rulers with blue-chip stock.
Lord, stay hidden in our midst.
Lord, do not answer our prayers.
Lord, do not reveal yourself.
Tease our reason with paradox.
Let imagination release us from ourselves
until touching every sacred body,
we find nothing left to believe
except the possibility of despair,
nothing left to pray except our work,
nothing more to hope except our love.
Lord, stay in winter places.
Shock our performances.
Make uncertain our journeys.

THOMAS

They made a saint of Thomas
because he cared enough to doubt.
He had to touch to believe, to suffer
dark nights sweating a question
until it poured light from his skin.
There are few temples in his name,
nor reconstructed theologies;
on the lips of priests, only scorn.
If in the darkness of an empty tomb
you still find someone searching,
looking in the corner for the shroud,
take his cold hand in yours,
and warm it with faith.

COUNTRY OF ILLUSIONS

There must be some mistake:
The road was here. At least
five years ago I thought
the road I sought was here.
But, straight ahead, as far as eye can see
there is no road,
and I must wait.

A WISE MAN

I saw a wise man
keep his silence
as he lay dreaming in a field
by small, dark streams
along a mountain road.
Now his eyes find mine
and laugh.

THE WIND

What must I do when the wind stalls
and the boat comes to a stop
near the dock?
Wait for me, whispers wind,
wait for me.
Be patient, be still and I shall come
just when you think I've gone.
Be ready, that's my advice,
for everything depends on that.

SEEING

If I want to see, I stay in the moment,
eyes closed and wait for God to come.
Sometimes there is nothing
but the sounds of waves
crashing on the Jersey shore
or a Vermont tree calling out to me
to pay attention.
And then I really see.

THE WEB OF LIFE

The web of life is woven, of which we are a part;
no one knows the reason why the horse before the cart.
Some say there is no moment when time began it all;
some say there is no ending, except a second Fall.
Black holes and quarks are symbols for things beyond our grasp,
we think by names we conquer but these shall never last.
Our theories have their experts, then fade away and die,
but you and I remain, my dear, as real, as deep, as sky.

THANK GOD

Thank God for foreign cars that get up to forty
miles per gallon on the road,
and for Henry Ford, too, who made us what we crave.
Thank you Lord for small cars,
for real American food of French fries and English fish,
for sugar and salt, Coke and Pepsi.
Thank you, God, for strong stomachs.
Thank you, God, for the balance of terror:
for bright, shiny tanks and smart bombs
which go right to the target.
Thank you God for the almighty Atom,
heir to your first son,
harbinger of our end.

AN ENGLISH GOD

An English God spreads marmalade upon his
buttered toast.
He drinks his tea at three. An English God, it's quite a boast,
is very much like me.
Just like a clock in perfect time he rules with equal hand,
the birds that fly, the snakes that crawl,
the bombs from upper air.
He spends his days above the earth, a decent chap at that;
becoming bald, a trifle fat, a bowler for his hat.
An English God is uninvolved in solving nasty quarrels,
and unperturbed, he keeps his nerve,
and always minds his morals.
An English God, though one in three,
is very much like me (thank God).

A NEW CHRIST?

They cry for a new Christ. Glad hosannas rise as the smoke
curls snake-like across the sky.
Surely the hour is at hand, the holy infusion near.
Weighed down by centuries of law, dark jewels
dangling from his neck, the prince of poverty and peace
stands before the kingdoms of this world
to acknowledge applause.
Outside the city gates another pale shepherd
retreats, unnoticed.
This new Christ understands the world this time.
He rides in pomp, and counts among his friends
the butchers and bankers of the planet.
When asked, he points to computer printouts
showing faith at an all-time high.

THE RED CHRIST

Alone, on the bare white wall, you hang there in silence.
What secret stirs within? Will no taunts make you
come down to talk?
Stay put, Red Christ, you are not my type.
Your eyes say it all.
Being without power is everything to God,
and means nothing to us.
Don't come down. You'll be rejected again.

THE QUAKER MEETING

The sense of the Meeting
was shattered by shotguns.
The birds felt the shells in the air,
but no one spoke of the disruption.
One must have faith
(did they hit a morning dove?).
No, one must know
(are the hunters coming closer?).
Leave the doors open
for they cannot shoot the Spirit
which comes and goes
in the blinking of an eye.
Leave the doors open
if you really have faith.

THE MURDER OF FAITH

He is not among you,
Not in the King James Bible
Nor a Bach chorus.
Not yet, you cannot find Him
In your stain glass prayers
Or capture Him with bread and wine
Or repeat your tamed words.
Reach back and recall the dying,
The abandonment and agony,
The scattered disciples,
The body revolted by time—
The murder of faith.

TAKE TIME

Take time, any time, to consider this:
Any time you will have no time
And will be nothing in time
Or be in some other time.
One moment you are here, another gone.
If you take this seriously,
Make some time your time.
Make every day a celebration
For honoring time itself.

ANGEL IN THE CHURCH

Last week I swear I saw an angel
in the church.
He had a sneaky smile and cracked
bad jokes about heaven.
He claimed to be a Cuban saved from Castro
(and sharks)by faith alone.
"So I know what fear is all about," he says,
dipping his hand through the table.
"Sharks, dictators, and churches
are much alike," he said.
I'm not sure he was joking.
He said he had a dream.
Now I know: Beware of angels bearing dreams,
especially if the message is for you.
"Don't be afraid," he said, as he pulled
a cigar from his coat pocket.
What could he mean not to be afraid?
What's there to fear around here
But stray bullets and drug dealers?
He stared and spoke clearly:
"You know fear like the back of your
hand, and so does everyone else."
I thought angels left the planet long ago
and only returned to Nashville from time to time.
They surely do not visit these cold, rational places.

Or as with empty tombs or burning bushes,
do they appear where least expected?
I don't know what to believe any longer.
I still hear his wings across the Gerber Room
and sense his presence on dim mornings
when the light bursts through the windows
like the hot fire of truth.
But I will tell you this: Now I walk fearless
past pimps and prostitutes, even greeting them
by name, because I hear right behind me
the footsteps of an angel and
the flutter of wings. And when I smell
the cigar, I am one fearless dude.

GROWING ALONE

Growing alone the cats keep you company
and purr at your touch.
Riding down the expressway, you look out
the window and know you are alone.
Now you expect nothing, want nothing,
have nothing.
Listen: Don't be sad. Exalt and dance.
Finally you can find yourself.

UNFINISHED BUSINESS

What has happened to you
matters little
in the flow of time
but everything.
Every thought will be remembered,
every deed recalled.
Everything matters
because it returns as love—
or unfinished business.

TIME

The loveliest things are
those that fade
into the shadow of the heart.
All drop beneath the autumn sun.
Yet surely something lives
when dying's done.
Deep, deep, within our sleep
there are more dreams to come.

THE MESSAGE OF THE LEAVES

The leaves race in circles before the fall wind,
hoping to beat winter one last time.
They dash as if some mad, swirling dance
might outwit the seasons.
But the truth is they will gather dust, too,
making soil for flowered spring.
The stone bears an epitaph: TRUST.
Trust in what? That change is certain?
That death is sure? Or, perhaps, what follows?
Soon snow will cover everything,
a white blanket placed upon the earth,
which sleeps until spring comes again
and we all awake.

ANOTHER INCONVENIENT TRUTH

It's like the warm wind dancing in the summer breeze
after a soaking and hot rainy night
giving the morning respite from the heat.
Or perhaps just a lonely chickadee waiting
to catch your eye.
Why not a vine flower blanched white and mingled
with an odor you've never smelled before
because you didn't take the time?
The news is dire—the ozone torn, the veil split,
the wars intense, people cruel with sacred lust.
But, oh, if I could feel once more the Spirit
which awakens one last hope that
we are made for more than extinction.

SEASONS

Brown and still on the ground, these dry leaves
huddle against the fall sun.
Pale winter is soon come, turning muted colors
into icy tombstones.
This seems the country of the dead, the horizons
of lost dreams, where ghosts, white with despair,
dance slowly across a gray sky.
But stand quietly and listen: Before your eyes,
Under the flesh, under the ground,
feel the roots gathering strength.
Be silent and reach down.
This is the whole of wisdom that the wind blows,
and the stars tell from distant galaxies.
This is the whole of wisdom that lost men give us
in dreams—and Lazarus died twice to find.
And now the roses grow before the country windows,
the hawks again circle overhead,
the fire bush catches flames to warm the hummingbird.
Smell the lilac, the fields.
Stand under the open heavens and sing praises
for another year—a time to begin anew.

THE END

Under new management, the heavens issue a memo:
"Pending further notice, all life is cancelled."
Workers weave in and out of offices, taking no time
to punch clocks or even bosses.
It's that time, friends, the great getting up morning, crunch time,
when Jesus will appear in the clouds
and take only a few of you home.
Get ready. I'm giving you fair warning:
 You've got only today to put your life in order.
What will you do when the dark rains fall and the
mountains crash to the seas, and the air turns bitter brown
with dust and debris?
You've got only today. Get ready.
Here it comes.
The End.

CREDITS

Written permission to use "The Seagull," "Lines Near Tintern Abbey, Wales," When It Comes Time to Die," given The Herald (www.universalist-her ald.net).

Written permission to use "A Psalm for Margaret," "A Prayer," "Thomas," "Unfinished Business," "Seasons," given by Friends Publishing Corporation, 2006 (www.friendsjournal.org).

Permission to use "At Easter Time," "In the Pastor's Study," granted by Richard L. Morgan, author.

"For Grandfather" appeared in "In the Shadow of Grace," Baker House Books, 2007.

"To My Father" appeared in "The God-Man of Galilee," Reston Publishing Company, 1983.

"To My Mother" appeared in the Anthology of Best American: Poems, 1992–1993.

"Crucifixion" published in "Prayers to Protest," Pudding House Publications, 1998.

ABOUT THE AUTHOR

John C. Morgan has been a writer for many years and now teaches philosophy and ethics at a community college. He is the author of many books, articles, and poems. This is his first volume of poetry.

www.ingramcontent.com/pod-product-compliance
Lightning Source LLC
Chambersburg PA
CBHW070947280326
41934CB00009B/2030